Liturgical Lay Ministers

A HANDBOOK FOR MINISTERS OF:

BREAD AND CUP
MUSIC
HOSPITALITY
WORD

REV. THOMAS J. ALLEN

TWENTY-THIRD PUBLICATIONS
P.O. Box 180   Mystic, CT 06355

ISBN 0-89622-152-0

Cover by Robert Maitland
Edited and designed by John G. van Bemmel
All photos by Thomas J. Allen

Contents

Introduction

This book is designed to be a handy one for pastoral leaders to place in the hands of liturgical lay ministers. It can be read privately by each minister, or with more advantage, used as a text for a parish-based class. The discussion questions at the end of each chapter will trigger some discussion among the ministers and help them to appreciate their ministry, one another's roles, and the needs of the parish. The priest-pastor or other staff member can easily lead the discussion, making modifications where necessary to fit unique parish situations.

The book can be used either to recruit new ministers or to enhance the ongoing ministry of present ministers.

The first two chapters deal with understanding "ministry" and "community," two essentials to any parish service. The subsequent chapters deal with the particular liturgical roles that have emerged in many places: Hospitality,

Word, Music, and Bread and Cup. The value in having all this succinctly stated under one cover is in having each minister appreciate the ministries of the others, so to enhance the whole.

Regional training programs for lay ministers may choose this book as one of several resources. It is not comprehensive, but it is cohesive. It is intended to be a good overview and provide an outline for further study.

Finally, the book can be used along with the six-part sound filmstrip program *Lay Ministries Training Program* by the same author and publisher. The chapters of the book correlate with the filmstrips.

Understanding Eucharistic Ministry

For most Catholics, Sunday Mass is the most significant religious event in their week, and they are used to recognizing their parish pastor or associate pastor in the central role as presider at the liturgy. In recent years, some parishioners have taken on the tasks of reading the Scripture passages and distributing holy Communion; this is in addition to the ushers and the organists that we knew in the past. All these tasks form the basis of the lay liturgical ministries—"lay" because they are done by certain members of the people of God, "liturgical" because they are done publicly at the assembly of the People of God, and "ministries" because they are recognized as authorized, stable functions that serve the people of God. The priest-presider has other ministers associated with him at Mass, each with his or her own role and function.

People need to understand this "teamwork" notion before they can be invited to take on one of the ministries. Most Catholics are accustomed to having the priest "say" the Mass and see other ministers as "helpers" for him. In a sense this is true, because the four lay liturgical ministries do help the presiding priest. But they also enhance the whole community's prayer by their own participation. As stable roles, the ministries go beyond "Mr. Smith helping Father"; rather they are the community's participation in the Lord's Supper: the presider's role (Father Martinez, today), the reader's role (Mr. Weber, today), the musician's role (Mrs. Sigl, today), the Bread and Cup minister's role (Miss Lensi, today), and the hospitality minister's role (Sr. Anita, today). The task of the present generation seems to be to move from "helping Father with Mass" to "taking part in the Lord's Supper according as we are called and gifted by God."

Christian people serve each other and the people of our society in a thousand ways. Keep in mind that here we are referring only to liturgical ministry, though, of course, much of what is said can be applied to public ministry outside the liturgy and to Christian service in general. For liturgy is the *celebration* of the ministry of God's people, not the whole of ministry itself. We gather on Sunday to celebrate the many calls and gifts from God that we have responded to throughout the week. We do it together and publicly, because God has formed us into a community of followers of his

Son. Our purpose is to praise and thank him through Jesus. The gathered community has its own roles and needs; hence, we have the liturgical ministries, headed by the presiding priest.

The Meaning of Ministry

A distinction can be made between "ministry" and "service." Although both English words translate the New Testament word "diakonia," the word "service" applies to the very broadest good work, as in Public Service, Military Service, Automobile Service Station, and, for Christians, Christian service. This is service done for the public, the military, for Christians, for anyone *on behalf of and in the name of Jesus Christ.* On the other hand, "ministry," in the singular, generic spelling, means good work

done consciously in the name of a particular Christian community. "Ministries" in the plural, specific sense, refers to the several roles that the particular community needs and authorizes. For Catholics, this authorization usually comes from the bishop or the pastor, speaking as the head of the community. It is in this last sense that we speak of the new lay liturgical "ministries."

No one should take a ministerial role upon himself or herself. The initiative comes from God ultimately, but is usually channeled through perceptive people. This is a subtle but very real happening! An individual notices that the quality of the celebration of Mass may be enhanced in a particular way, for example, by welcoming newcomers to church. He or she then talks it over with other members and realizes that they have the gifts to be Ministers of Hospitality. The individual discusses it with the parish leaders, including the pastor, and they begin to call the gifted ones into the ministry. With training and consciousness raising over a period of time, a corps of Ministers of Hospitality emerges from the community, gifted and called by God!

The freedom to say yes or no is always part of the call (or "vocation") and the period of time in one particular ministry may be quite changeable depending upon the other "calls" in one's life (see Acts 6:1-6). The process of being called within a community is accompanied by reflection, prayer for guidance, and true freedom. Also, the art of encouraging and coordinating volunteers is helpful, and by custom the parish priest can contribute immensely to the process of enabling volunteers to join the ministries.

Ministers enjoy doing their particular ministry and benefit from the other ministries as does the whole community. In the past, the priest-presider had assumed almost all the ministerial roles (perhaps by default), but today each minister has a respect for the gifts and call of the others. Since the ministries are separate and unique, an individual shouldn't take on more than one ministry at a given time, unless in emergency. This leaves room for other gifted people to be called into the more public liturgical ministries, and so enhance the whole community's prayer.

Let us describe each of the four eucharistic ministries and say something about the requirements for each.

Minister of Hospitality

Hospitality is a much-needed gift in many Catholic assemblies. Partly because of the excessive size of some parishes and partly because of an exaggerated sense of piety, many Catholics do not greet each other in a friendly manner upon arriving at church. More unfortunately, the Sign of Peace, which is properly a profound reconciliation just before Communion, has become in many places a greeting. As good as it is, it points up the need for true hospitality at the beginning of Mass.

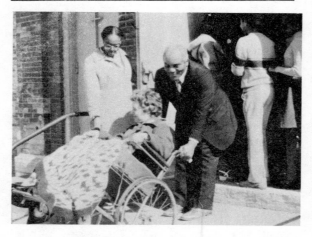

Designating a corps of persons as Ministers of Hospitality in no way satisfies the need for a general air of hospitality in the assembly. The Ministers set the tone for the rest. The priest-presider often speaks with people before and after the ceremony, and during the ceremony his attitude of warmth conveys "permission" for all to meet and celebrate in Christ. The Ministers of the Word, Bread and Cup, and Music convey an attitude of conviviality while carrying out their particular roles. But each of these other ministries has a distinct thrust. Some designated persons must care directly for the community during its gathering. These are the Ministers of Hospitality, or "ushers" as they were once known.

These ministers are friendly people, attracted to all age groups, nationalities, and to both sexes. Their faith enables them to see Christ's presence in individuals and in the gathered community. They appreciate the faith of our separated brothers and sisters. They can handle emergency situations with courage and aplomb. They carry a dignity about themselves, even when performing needed menial tasks.

Minister of the Word

The proclamation of the Word of God is an integral part of the liturgy. Even in silence the assembly meditates upon the Word proclaimed. The remembrance of the Lord's Supper is done in word, gesture, song, and with the elements of bread and wine. Even though the whole Mass is a proclamation of the Word of God, the cycle of readings from Scripture form the core of the Liturgy of the Word. The priest or deacon, ordained as "heralds of the Word," proclaim the gospel and preach the homily. Other Ministers of the Word present the readings from the Hebrew Scriptures and from the Christian epistles. They read aloud from the Lectionary the texts indicated for that day, so that everyone may hear and understand. The reason for having more than one "Minister of the Word" is to enrich the community's faith by the witness of more than one reader; for proclaiming the Word of God is an act of faith in him who is the Word of God made flesh. Hence, generally speaking, several Ministers of the Word are preferable to one. The variety of voices enhances the ability

of people to listen attentively. The cantor, as a
Minister of Music, adds much with a musical
rendition of the Word as found in the Responsorial Psalm.

Ministers of the Word love the Bible. They
read it privately, join Bible study groups, and
are eager to share with others the riches they
have discovered. They have strong, clear voices
and are willing to stand before an assembly of
believers and proclaim God's Word.

Minister of the Bread and Cup

The Mass is a sacramental meal. Those who
serve the holy food are like table waiters who
really enjoy serving food to others. Deeply con-
vinced of the real presence of Jesus Christ in the
bread and wine, these Ministers of the Bread
and Cup convey their appreciation of this great
gift to each believer who comes forward to
receive it. With deliberate words and gestures,
the Ministers give the sacred food for life to each
individual.

The Ministers of the Bread and Cup are
generous people who can care for each communicant as Jesus himself cares for them. The
gesture of giving is a personal act, an act between two believers who realize Jesus' presence.

Minister of Music

Music played and sung during the Mass is a very
special part of the Ministry of the Word. Music
as a human art form conveys meanings beyond

words to the feelings of a person. It unites the people of God in one voice of response to the Word.

The Minister of Music is a musician whose deep faith is the key reason for leading or performing a musical prayer within the assembly. The appreciation of beauty as a gift from God is celebrated by the faith-filled musician. He or she leads the assembly in sung prayer, the very texts of the Mass, and hymns. The Minister of Music helps a variety of people to deepen their appreciation of beautiful music as a form of prayer. He or she is flexible and constantly listens to the assembly to see whether their prayer is actually being enhanced by the music.

God does call people for certain responsibilities. To find out whether he is calling you to one of these for ministries, take the following steps:

1. Ask God to make it clear to you through the Spirit.

2. Suggest to those who love you that you are considering this step.

3. Listen carefully to their responses.

4. Approach others who are already liturgical ministers and ask them to share their experiences.

5. Approach your pastor or one designated by him to learn what is needed in your parish.

6. Make a choice based on the previous steps, of the ministry you will serve in.

7. Seek the proper training.

8. In the course of the training, be aware of your own particular talents, skills, and preferences. Thank God for them.

Questions
for Reflection
and Discussion

What do you think of the reasons people give not to be a eucharistic minister? Do the reasons seem valid in themselves? What can a parish do to encourage people to volunteer? To recruit more effectively?

Do people in your parish look to their parish as a place to belong? Why? Why not? Does your parish offer people an opportunity to have fuller participation and service at Mass?

How does "service" differ from "ministry"? Do you agree with this distinction? Why? Why not?

In regard to eucharistic ministers, how would you assess your parish's needs? In what precise ways will these ministers help to improve Sunday Mass?

Have you already decided whether you wish to be a eucharistic minister or not? If you wish to be one, then which ministry appeals to you? For which one are you best qualified? Have you discussed these decisions with other potential ministers? With parish leaders? With your family?

Is the Eucharist usually celebrated in your parish in such a way that it is likely to be a faith-filled experience for all? Do you see yourself, and the other ministers, contributing to this goal? How?

Understanding the Worshipping Community

People approach involvement in lay eucharistic ministry from a variety of backgrounds. Their previous experiences in the Church color other understanding of what they are to do and why they are to do it. An important part of a training program is to help a person understand his or her proper place in the ministries. To do this well, we need to appreciate the diversity and variety of experiences that people have of the Church.

Models of Church

In his book *Models of the Church* Rev. Avery Dulles, S.J., gives us a helpful outline of different views of the Church. He calls them "models," that is, mental constructions of how the Church exists for us. His models are:

1. The Church as community
2. The Church as servant

3. The Church as herald
4. The Church as institution
5. The Church as sacrament

Depending on the prevailing model of the Church in our minds and hearts, our response to the needs of the Church will vary.

For most Catholics the parish in which they grew up, and the parish in which they as adults live, contribute the most to their own image of the Church. For example, if those parishes operated mostly out of the "institution" model, the dominant model will be, for them, institutional. The other four models will affect them to a lesser degree.

It is helpful for a ministry candidate to discover for himself or herself which is the dominant model or combination of models that affects his or her image of the Church, and consequently his or her attitude toward the ministries. It will also help in selecting the proper ministry. A pastor or counselor should help in this decision process.

Here are some guidelines, based on these models, for candidates to use in the selection of the proper, suitable ministry:

1. The Church as community. Some people want their parish to be fairly small and close-knit, with a degree of intimacy in Jesus Christ. Everyone knows everyone else, at least by name and face. The liturgies should be evidently joyful, like a family gathering. Each person's gifts are recognized and used.

Candidates with this model of the Church serve as Ministers of Hospitality and Ministers of Music, both of which contribute directly to a sense of oneness, warmth, and friendliness.

2. The Church as servant. Some people want their parish to lead the town or neighborhood in changing unchristian situations and in helping unfortunate people. The parish should serve the Kingdom of God, bringing it slowly into this world by their selfless service.

   Candidates with this model of the Church serve as Ministers of Bread and Cup, feeding the hungry and thirsty, and Ministers of Hospitality, caring for the disabled, the sick, etc. during Mass.

3. The Church as herald. Some people want their parish to be more Bible oriented and more evangelistic. The Church presents the Word of God in a courageous and authentic manner so that everyone really gets the full message of Jesus.

   Candidates with this model of the Church serve as Ministers of the Word and Ministers of Music, especially cantors.

4. The Church as institution. Many people want their parish to be very stable with clear rules, an established membership, and clear, official leadership. Others may join by becoming converts to the established criteria, and

members may leave when they no longer agree with the official position or any given point.

Candidates with this model of the Church join the ministries when they find that the membership is diminishing, the leadership is old and few in numbers, or funds are lacking. Since the pope and bishop have agreed that people should take more active responsibilities, they are quite willing to help sustain the Church, which was founded upon a rock by Jesus himself. They serve in all four ministries, especially in a crisis.

5. The Church as sacrament. Many people see the parish as the place where they can go to receive the sacraments, to be in touch with God's grace in a world full of conflicting

signs. The Church is a sign itself of God's presence among us. The sacraments work for us at critical times in our lives when we need God. The rituals speak to us clearly of God's ultimate care for us.

Candidates with this model of Church want their parish to provide many Masses so that everyone can be in touch with God. The church building must be beautiful and well-kept and be prominent in their town or neighborhood. Candidates serve as Ministers of Bread and Cup and as Ministers of Hospitality who care for the upkeep of the building.

Keep in mind that no single model of the Church really exists anywhere. In fact, your parish is a mixture, a complex reality with many levels of meaning—a mystery! But a mystery full of the Spirit of God. We believe that Christ is constantly with the Church and that his Spirit has guided us since its beginning. Many changes have taken place over the centuries, and we are yet in the midst of another enormous change in the life of the Church.

History of Liturgical Ministries

From the beginning of Christianity, the form of the Lord's Supper grew with the culture, theology, and the numbers of people. In the first century and longer, the house-churches of the pauline communities were hosted by the wealthy owner who provided hospitality. The structure of the Liturgy of the Word was borrowed from the synagogue service and the Liturgy of the Eucharist derived from the passover meal. Most of the ministerial functions followed those structures: someone to read and comment; someone to tell the Lord's words and deeds at the Last Supper; someone to break the bread and pour the wine. The form followed the function.

After Constantine's Edict of Milan in 313 AD, the number of believers and the number of church buildings increased dramatically, and a whole new class of ministries developed to care for converts and for the buildings. The assemblies grew large, necessitating permanent responsibilities on the part of many.

In time, the church became an institution, and the responsibilities gradually became set into stable offices; a clerical, caretaking class of Christians emerged. Bishops (overseers), presbyters (elders), and deacons (servants) headed a growing Church. Even though many ordinary Christians had important responsibilities in the Church, slowly through the early Middle Ages only those men who were tonsured, that is, made clerics, could hold office in the Church. Most of the functions associated with the celebration of the Eucharist were absorbed by the main minister, the priest or bishop. Deacons all but disappeared. Lay people no longer sang nor received Communion. Eventually, Mass was celebrated privately or at a great physical distance from the people.

In 1972 Pope Paul VI reversed the medieval rule that restricted all the eucharistic ministries to clerics. His instruction, *Ministeria Quaedam,* called for the restoration of needed ministries; he wanted all Catholics to be able to engage in them. Certain of these ministries are liturgical, and two of these liturgical ministries are named in the document: lector and acolyte. National conferences of bishops are to develop and name the other needed ministries.

Lector and acolyte, as stable and universal liturgical ministries, have one important restriction: only men may be installed officially. In the United States, however, this restriction is lifted in practice by other legislation (#66 Appendix to the General Instruction, February, 1971; and U.S. Indult March, 1971) so that women may also read the Scriptures and distribute Communion.

In a lay ministry training program, the term "Minister of . . ." is used consistently to name the ministers, to provide clarity. Also, in dioceses where the bishop chooses to, he may informally recognize women and men alike as "Ministers of Word" and "Ministers of Bread and Cup."

Sacred Time

Liturgical ministers need to have an appreciation of the pattern of the Church week and year as the rhythm of our life in Christ. Each Sunday is a remembrance of Jesus' resurrection; that is why we term Sunday the "Lord's Day" and take part in a Eucharist celebration that day. It is the high point of our week when we are assembled in faith for Mass. Each week we go forth renewed and strengthened for the role and task that God has put into our lives.

The liturgical year is a pattern of remembered events that have made us God's people: the saving events of Jesus' life, death, and resurrection. Christians are people who remember what God has done and live in the hope of greater deeds. Each year we have Advent awaiting Christmas, Lent preparing for Holy Week and Easter, the ordinary time when the Spirit guides us after Pentecost. The Feasts of our Lord, Mary, and the saints bring to mind important events, just as we remember the national holidays and a joyful family gathering.

Sacred Space

The church building is more than a convenient place to gather. Although multi-purpose auditoriums are sometimes used for religious gatherings, the parish church contains so much more. The community of young and old have gathered here time and time again and left their marks. More than a museum of memories, the building is like the skin over the body of believers holding them together and protecting them. In the church, too, is reserved the Sacrament of the Eucharist, for Communion of the sick and for private prayer. This sacred space is decorated with time-honored symbols of faith and in a special way speaks to us of Christ living in his people. Ministers of the Eucharist feel at home in this church building. They care for it with the whole parish community.

Planning for Mass

The church building has been provided by our predecessors; the yearly cycle of celebrations is marked out for us. Ministers of the Eucharist may feel they only need to do their job when the time comes.

No, a necessary component for high quality liturgy is planning, long-range and short-range planning. First, short range.

The church building must be readied:

1. Ventilation, heat, light, doors unlocked

2. Books, bells, wine, water, altar breads, microphone
3. Musical instruments, song books, bulletins
4. Texts and homily

The ministers must be ready:

1. Music and readings practiced
2. Homily prepared
3. Ministers properly attired
4. Special groups (for example, for baptisms) prepared.

Short-range planning is easily done by a few dedicated people. Too often it is the only planning done. Long-range planning requires much more.

1. In many places, the services of a priest must be obtained before anything else. Priest personnel planning is fast becoming not simply a diocesan concern, but a concern for each parish.
2. Provision for the upkeep of the church and procurement of needed supplies: wine, breads, candles, vessels, cloths, and clothing. Books, instruments, flowers, banners, statues, etc.
3. Recruitment of needed ministers
4. Training of needed ministers
5. Assignment and scheduling of needed ministers
6. Coordination of the theme, the readings, the musical texts, the decorations, the homily, the announcements, the bulletin, etc.

7. Evaluation of previous liturgies with an eye for improvement.
8. Ongoing education of the ministers.

In many places long-range planning is done by a liturgy planning group that meets with regularity and is accountable to the parish council and the pastor. Sometimes a sub-group will take responsibility for a special feast day, or liturgy planning groups will plan all Sunday Masses on a rotational basis throughout the year.

Questions
for Reflection
and Discussion

Is your dominant view of the Church like one of these expressed here? Which one? Is it a different view? How would you express it?

Is your dominant view of the Church like one of these five "models"? Which one? Does it differ in some ways? Is there another model of the Church not expressed here? Which model would you say your parish is like?

Do you think all five models of the Church are included in, and can be reconciled with, this Second Vatican Council view of the Church?

Why does the way you view your parish and the Church generally influence your decision to be a eucharistic minister or not, to be one kind of minister and not another? What does the history of lay participation in the Mass tell you about being a eucharistic minister today?

Do you agree or disagree with the view that the way Ministers of the Eucharist view the congregation will have an important effect on the quality of their ministry? What are your reasons? How do you view the congregation in your parish?

Why is a eucharistic minister's appreciation of the church building important to his or her work? How does the building affect this work? Affect the celebration of Mass?

Have you thought about your ministry quotient, your talents and readiness for a particular ministry? If you think God calls you to eucharistic ministry, to which form of it do you feel called? Do your inclinations to one form or another coincide with your talents?

Concerning the details to be planned for Mass, what would you add to those mentioned? Concerning those who should be part of the liturgy planning group, who would you include? As a minister, in what areas of planning Mass would you like to participate? Why?

The Minister

of Hospitality

The gentlemen who traditionally have served as ushers in Catholic churches have not often thought of themselves as Ministers of Hospitality. More often they were considered necessary to take up the money collection and to keep order if an emergency arose. The modern Minister of Hospitality incorporates the best of the functions of the past and adds some contemporary functions.

The Minister of Hospitality is related to the former Minor Order of Porter, or Doorkeeper. Since Pope Paul VI's *Ministeria Quaedam* in 1972, the Minor Orders are replaced by the lay ministries, which in fact had been done most often by laypeople anyway. In one sense, Church law had caught up with Church practice. But the added element is what is important, hospitality.

Hospitality helps people feel "at home" and welcomed while they are at church. It is as essential for regular church-goers as it is for newcomers, for it is the first step in the gathering or the assembly of believers, which we call "Church." A sense of community (*koinonia*) is a prerequisite for community prayer.

In the Judeo-Christian tradition, hospitality has had a long history. From the desert hospitality of the semitic tribes, to the doorkeepers at the Jerusalem Temple, to the hosts and hostesses of the pauline Churches (for example, Lydia of Thystira, Acts 16:14-15), to the custodian class in the post-Constantinian Church, hospitality has had its designated ministers.

The Need for the Hospitality Minister

It would be a mistake to relate this ministry solely to the needs of the church building itself. Just as a homemaker deals with the details of many things to make the house a home, so do Ministers of Hospitality deal with physical details to make the building a hospitable church. But the focus is on the people who gather there. Ministers care for people, above all, and secondarily for the building (Martha and Mary, Luke 10:41), for the presence of Christ is first revealed in the community. "Where two or three are gathered in my name, I am there in the midst of them" (Matthew 18:19).

Ministers of Hospitality are persons of faith who can perceive Jesus present in the gathering community. They welcome people at the doorway, because entering the church building and signing the cross with holy water upon one's body is a dramatic recall of our baptism. It is fitting for the Minister of Hospitality to represent the community right there where a "mini-baptism" is being acted out. The church-goer is crossing over from secular time and space into sacred time and space. A believing Minister of Hospitality is there to greet him or her in Christ's name. A seasonal greeting and a warm smile complete the entry of the Christian into his home parish, or better, his parish home. In large churches where many people gather, this may be the only time a minister can deal one-to-one with the parishioners.

The attitude of hospitality "rubs off" on people and creates an atmosphere of quiet joy and acceptance. Having many Ministers of Hospitality doesn't eliminate the need for each church-goer to be communicative with others; it does encourage and support them in their acts of warmth and kindness. As time goes on, the Ministers of Hospitality will no longer stand out because of their friendliness, for the whole community will be sharing a sense of hospitality.

Some nameplate or special garb is helpful to provide immediate recognition of the Ministers of Hospitality, for example, blazers for the men, long hostess skirts or lapel flowers for the women. This quick recognition helps newcomers to feel "officially" greeted, and the old-timers to realize the special ministry of their friends and neighbors.

In various times and places, Ministers of Hospitality have been known by others names: sextant, sacristan, janitor, people with the responsibility of preparing the building for God's people. The bell-ringer called people to prayer by ringing out the time of day. The collector of funds gathered the money offerings of people. In certain parts of the world, leaders of "base communities" bring their small groups to church to meet and pray with Christians from many other such groups. These "animators" enliven the faith of many people by their ministry. The Rite of Christian Initiation of Adults (RCIA) envisions sponsors of catechumens as Ministers of Hospitality who quite literally introduce a prospective member to the community. Finally, there are those who go out from the assembly to contact the sick and the shut-in members. Oftentimes these are

Ministers of Bread who bring holy Communion .

One of the greatest acts of hospitality, of course, is not a liturgical ministry at all; it is the ministry of evangelization where believers go forth to invite non-believers to join (or rejoin) the faith community. They create an atmosphere of openness and trust where someone may receive the gift of faith from God. These evangelizers fill the banquet feast by going out to the highways and byways to seek out all kinds of people. They return to the gathering to be renewed in their life in Christ.

The Hospitality Minister's Tasks

The building:
1. Arrive at church prior to everyone else.
2. Prepare money baskets and bags.
3. Set up the table for gifts of bread and wine
4. Check ventilation, heat, and light.
5. Check with priest-celebrant for any special instructions.

The people:
1. Ring the tower bells at the proper time.
2. Greet people at the doors.
3. Help the handicapped and the elderly, especially on stairs.
4. Escort or "seat" people from front to back, introducing strangers and placing friends in proximity to each other.
5. Where it is customary, select the gift-presentors and cue them on their task.

The liturgy:
1. Seat latecomers unobtrusively.

2. Participate by word and posture in the action of the Mass.
3. Be aware of any emergencies or special needs, for example, a cup of water to a coughing individual.
4. Direct the smooth formation of processions.
5. Take up the money collection during a pause in the liturgy, for example, after the general intercessions or during a period of reflection.
6. If customary, present the collected money to the priest or deacon, or place it near the altar.
7. Assist in the free flow of people to the front for the Communion procession.
8. Alert the Ministers of Bread and Cup if someone unable to approach the front wants to receive Communion.

After the liturgy:

1. Pass out parish bulletins or newspapers and say your goodbye ("God by ye") as people leave.
2. If a gathering or extension of the Eucharist occurs after Mass, encourage people to attend and accompany them to the hall.
3. Straighten up the church building: kneelers, hymnals, extra chairs, bathrooms, vestibules.
4. Put the collection money in a safe place.
5. Turn off lights, close windows, and so on.

The "hospitality hour" after Mass is, of course, an extension of the Eucharist. All the ministers can greet informally the people they have served. While other Ministers of Hospitality serve the food and drink, the liturgical ministers may be relieved of their responsibilities for liturgy and simply enjoy the company of their faith-filled friends.

The Hospitality Ministers' Room

Furnishings:

1. Mirror
2. Coat rack
3. Small desk or bookshelf
4. Chair for the sick
5. Stretcher or cot
6. Blanket
7. Oxygen tank
8. Fire extinguisher and cut-off valve for sprinkler system
9. Telephone and emergency numbers
10. Lost and found storage

Supplies:

1. Bulletin information
2. Drinking cups—water available
3. Facial tissue
4. "Reserved" signs
5. Pencils
6. Special money envelopes
7. First-aid supplies
   a. Smelling salts
   b. Aspirin
   c. Alka Seltzer
   d. Band Aid
   e. Safety pins
   f. Vomit absorbent material
   g. Room deodorant spray

Questions
for Reflection
and Discussion

Is the description of the spirit of warmth and friendliness expressed here like that in your parish? How do you think this spirit might be improved?

To what extent do the Ministers of Hospitality in your parish help to turn the Sunday obligation into a Sunday privilege and joy? Do they help people feel that they belong to your parish? Do you think that this is an essential part of the hospitality ministry?

Do you think it is accurate to say that people come to Mass to be renewed, up-lifted, and to have deep contact with God and with one another? What might a Minister of Hospitality do to help people attain this goal?

Is there something you would add to the list of duties of a Minister of Hospitality? Is there something you think should not belong to his or her duties? What? Is this list a close portrayal of

the ministers in your parish? In what areas is improvement called for? Is there enough attention paid to individual needs?

What are the reasons why your parish has (or does not have) a hospitality hour? Why do you agree or disagree with these reasons? What would you suggest to help your parish maintain an atmosphere of a warm and loving community celebrating the Eucharist?

The Minister
of the Word

The great privilege and burden of reading the Word of God to his people is the central function of this important ministry. It is a privilege because a lector stands in the long tradition of the prophets as proclaimers of the Word; it is a burden because the lector is also the first hearer of what he or she reads. The layperson who reads the first two Scripture selections at Mass shares the total Ministry of the Word with many others: bishops, presbyters, deacons, scripture scholars and teachers, theologians, evangelists, missionaries, catechists, cantors, and parents. In the broadest sense, each Christian is a minister of the Word made flesh, Jesus Christ, because we are all to make him known to the nations. This is the foremost ministry in the Church, and it comes to every Christian with baptism into the Body of Christ.

At the liturgical moment when the believers are seated and attentive, however, the whole focus of the Ministry of the Word is upon the one who holds the Sacred Book to read. In a specific sense, the lector makes the Word of God living and active in the midst of the assembly—he is God's contemporary prophet! But within the liturgy the proclamation of the Word is also done by other ministers. The presbyter or deacon proclaims the gospel selection and preaches the homily. The previous two readings, usually one from the Hebrew Scriptures and one from the epistles, set the scene and prepare the believers. The relationship of the lector's task to the presbyter's or deacon's is that of John the Baptist to Jesus Christ. John prepared the way for Jesus. The people are standing ready for the gospel when the lector has finished his task.

Most people in our churches are literate, and in many places, hand missals or disposable missalettes are placed in the pews for people to read from. This custom should never be allowed to detract from the lector's task of communicating and witnessing to what he or she has communicated. The fact that the printed word is so readily available to our people should not diminish the freshness and conviction with which the Word of God is read aloud. The plentiful printed copies must enhance this communication process or else be discarded.

The Minister and Faith

The key to the lector's role is "witness." What is read must first be understood, believed, and then proclaimed. Good public reading is a necessary skill, but it is not enough. The lector must convey his or her own belief. As true as this is, it may seem to be a heavy burden for a lector, especially if a congregation has been lulled into a half-hearing lethargy by years of routinely poor reading or by a sound system of poor quality. It is a heavy burden but it is not borne solely by the lector, because communication is a two-way process. The listeners have an essential part – listening in such a way that the lector notes their belief. Their witness takes the form of an active and attentive listening and then a response (the Responsorial Psalm). When lector and listeners mutually witness their faith, Jesus, the Word of God, becomes present in the assembly.

In the total Ministry of the Word, there are clear and important distinctions. The role of a theologian is not the same as the role of the bishop, for example. Within the liturgy, too, the distinction of roles is important for good order. Lectors do not double up by also distributing Communion or giving the general intercessions if a deacon is present, or reciting the psalm if a cantor is present to sing it. It is even preferable to have two lectors, one for each reading, than simply one lector for two readings. With two, there are two people witnessing their faith, plus a change in voice and face.

There is a further distinction between lector and reader. Both are Ministers of the Word, but the lector is officially installed in the ministry by the bishop, whereas the readers are "other faithful who by a temporary appointment are to read the Sacred Scripture in liturgical celebrations" (*Ministeria Quaedam*). The official installation is open only to men. Consequently, in some places, the local bishop *unofficially* recognizes men and women alike as Ministers of the Word, after suitable training. Generally these trained Ministers of the Word, in turn, lead and train temporary readers from their parishes.

Studying God's Word

The Minister of the Word develops a great love for the Bible and has a habit of private Bible study. Many have a well-worn copy of the Bible for their personal use and have gathered other biblical resource books, perhaps a subscription

to a magazine about biblical themes as well. Sometimes the group of readers in a parish form themselves into a Scripture study group and share their insights, their prayer, and their resources. Some seek college and seminary classes in Sacred Scripture, or attend workshops. The interfaith contact with Protestants and Jews often opens up unappreciated facets of the richness of the Bible.

Proper English pronunciation cannot be taken for granted. A lector should use a dictionary whenever there is a doubt about it. Biblical names and places can be checked in a biblical dictionary. Many times the beginning reader is unaware of mispronunciations and, therefore, should practice aloud for the critique of another person. Another good reason for practicing aloud with someone else present is the wide variation in electronic sound systems and in acoustical quality in church buildings. That person can tell you whether you are coming over the system well or not. The echo quality of some large churches requires that a lector read quite slowly. Good diction and articulation also take practice, and the honest opinions of a friendly critic is helpful. Deep breathing in a relaxed way helps the voice to sound powerful yet unstrained at the same time. The key to good reading quality is rehearsal in the church building with the amplifier on, and a competent person to serve as critic.

One cannot possibly convey meaning without first understanding the meaning for

oneself! Oftentimes it is helpful to read the whole book or chapter from the Bible from which the selection is taken. This gives the lector the context of the passage. The lector should privately read the gospel selection, too, to see how it relates in meaning with the first and second reading.

The Bible is made up of history, poetry, laws, succinct "sayings," songs, and parables. What type of literature is in today's selection? The lector must read it accordingly. In many subtle inflections and modulations of voice the reader displays his or her understanding of the text. People may not expect dramatic, interpretative reading, but are generally excited when the meaning comes through to them with just one hearing. The controlled enthusiasm of a well-prepared lector elicits a grateful response from God's people.

The Minister of the Word may fittingly wear a white robe. There are many reasons for this, though not all observers would agree. The white robe or alb is in fact the baptismal robe with which we all "put on Christ Jesus." Every baptised person is entitled to "dress up" for the banquet of the Lord's Supper in his special garb. The Ministers of the Word (and the Ministers of Bread and Cup) wear the robe as a sign that they are carrying out their special baptismal call. The dignity of the robe adds another note of a special event. On the practical level, distinctions of fashion and fad are easily overcome, which may offend those who have a quick eye for economic or gender status. Costuming has a deep meaning in our cultural and anthropological roots. Street clothes, although acceptable, may eventually prove to be banal. The Minister of the Word should follow the custom of the parish, while keeping an eye on these values.

Questions
for Reflection
and Discussion

What is your understanding of what it means when Scripture is proclaimed at Mass? Is the proclamation of Scripture a faith-filled experience for you?

Are the Ministers of the Word in your parish effective? Are they good Ministers of the Word? Do you think you are or will be a good minister? Why? What other qualifications would you add to those listed?

Which of the tools suggested in this section does your parish provide for lectors? Are there others you think the Ministers of the Word would use with profit? Do you agree that "the more you know about Scripture in general and a passage in particular, the more effective a reader you will be"? What are your reasons? How does a reader's knowledge and faith affect his or her performance? Affect the assembly?

Do the readers in your parish seem to be prepared for their ministry? In what respects does improvement seem called for? What suggestions for preparation would you add to those mentioned? What do you think would help you to be fully prepared?

Does the actual procedure in your parish differ in any significant way from what is described here? Is this difference worth discussing with parish leaders? Why? Is the procedure in your parish effective? Understood by all?

Would you add any other norms on reading well in public to those presented here? What are they? Do the Ministers of the Word in your parish have the opportunity to practice reading in church? To practice with other readers? Describe your feelings about the statement that you are privileged to announce, "This is the Word of the Lord," as it applies to you.

The Minister

of the Bread and Cup

Until recently the handling of holy Communion was reserved to bishops, priests, and deacons. In the Catholic Church in the United States today, it is the usual practice for believers to receive the sacred bread in their hands or on their tongues, to receive the sacred wine on certain occasions by means of a cup in their hands, and for certain believers to be designated as Ministers of Communion. These adjustments in Church law and practice are all designed to restore a more proximate and frequent access to the Eucharist. The twentieth century has seen many changes in eucharistic practice – all in the direction of greater availability of holy Communion to the believing community.

The minimum age for first reception of Communion was lowered to the tender age of seven. The fasting from food and drink prior to receiving Communion was relaxed. "Full participation" in the Mass came to include reception of Communion. American Catholics began to receive Communion weekly at the Sunday Eucharist. Communion was allowed a second time in the same day when people had occasion to take part in another liturgy. The reception of sacred wine from the cup was reintroduced after centuries of being the exclusive privilege of the priest.

As the Church returned to the fuller eucharistic practice of the premedieval times, the greater numbers of communicants led to some practical problems. The time for serving Communion to the assembly became disproportionately long, especially when both species (bread and wine) were distributed. The restoration of Communion-in-the-hand, quite late in the reforms in this country, enabled a faith-exchange between minister and recipient; consequently, the time got even longer. In a few places the reforms were seriously impaired by the time factor. Efficiency and speed sometimes became the benchmark of suburban Catholic parishes. The size of the parking lot dictated the quality of liturgical prayer. Something had to be done.

A Developing Ministry

In March 1971, Pope Paul VI gave permission to the bishops of the United States to authorize certain lay people to help in the distribution of holy Communion (*Custos Fidei*). They are called "extraordinary ministers of the Eucharist" – extraordinary because the ordinary ministers continue to be the deacon, priest, and bishop. These extraordinary ministers may include women and men. A year later, Pope Paul VI restored the ministry of acolyte, which included the functions of the extraordinary minister of the Eucharist, for the whole Church (*Ministeria Quaedam*). This officially installed ministry of acolyte excluded women, however. To further complicate matters, most of the functions traditionally performed by altar boys were reassigned to the adult acolyte.

What is emerging in the United States out of this recent legislation is the role of the Minister of Bread and Cup. These are men and women of faith who serve the holy Eucharist with both species to the assembly. Their names are enrolled by the bishop, and they are "recognized" publicly in a special ceremony either by the bishop or by the pastor in the presence of the assembly. They have been specially trained for this ministry either in their home parish or in a diocesan program. Those with more extensive training minister at the altar and assist the deacon and the priest. They are entrusted with exposition of the Blessed Sacrament, but not with blessing the people.

In some places the duties of the altar boys are absorbed by the adult ministers; in other places young boys and girls assist the adult acolytes by carrying the sacramentary, the candles, the cross, the incense, and so forth. Clearly, as adult ministers take on their proper role, the children have less to do and take a more peripheral place. Instead of "Father and the altar boys" up front, contemporary assemblies see the presiding priest surrounded by many adult ministers from the community. Perhaps the teapot tempest over "altar girls" will simply disappear by not having the liturgical ministries done by children at all, except in liturgies planned especially by and for children.

Those who bring holy Communion to the sick and shut-ins are a second group of ministers. These men and women are specially trained to minister to the sick. They lead the "Rite of Communion for the Sick" in the presence of the sick person and his or her family and friends, giving holy Communion to those gathered. They obtain the sacred bread from the tabernacle in church outside of Mass, or at the time of their own Communion they may place sufficient hosts in the pyx (small container) to serve to the sick. These Communion ministers to the sick and shut-ins do not function during Mass.

A third group of Communion ministers should be mentioned. A relative or close friend of a sick or shut-in person may bring Communion to that person for the duration of their illness, upon receiving permission from their pastor. This is not a ministry in the stable sense; it receives no public commissioning. It is a laudable Christian service. The "Rite of Communion for the Sick" is used.

Where sufficient Ministers of the Bread and Cup are doing their ministry during Mass, the duration of Communion distribution is proportionate to the rhythm of the rest of the Mass. It is preferable to have more ministers than to have only a few hurrying through long lines of communicants. Generally two Ministers of the Cup would do for each Minister of the Bread, to keep the lines flowing deliberately and smoothly. A variety of persons as ministers also enhances the faith-witness of each to the people of the assembly.

The Ministers' Role

Ministers of the Bread assist the priest and deacon in the breaking of the bread, during the Lamb of God prayer. At the same time, the Ministers of the Cup fill small cups from the large cups or carafes used to contain the sacred wine. Each receives both species of Communion from another minister, usually the celebrant, and then all move to their assigned places to serve the people. The people approach the Minister of the Bread first, who says "The Body of Christ" to each one in turn. The response is simply "Amen." After consuming the bread, the individual may approach the Minister of the Cup, who says "The Blood of Christ"; the response is again "Amen." Then the minister hands the cup to the individual who drinks a sip. The minister then wipes the edge of the cup with a purificator (small white napkin), and the recipient returns to his or her place.

These mechanics must be practiced a few times before actually performing the ministry.

The emphasis, of course, is not on the mechanical aspects, but upon the shared faith of the two believers who meet in the Lord. After all the people are served, the Ministers of the Cup consume any sacred wine that remains. They then rinse the cup with water and wipe it dry. This process may take place after the Mass is over. The Ministers of the Bread place the remaining sacred bread in the ciborium (a container with a lid) inside the tabernacle, cleanse their fingers with water in an ablution cup and purificator (or just the purificator), and return to their places until the end of Mass. If no deacon is present, one of the Ministers of the Bread and Cup may remove all the vessels from the altar to a side table or to the sacristy.

Ministers of Bread and Cup wear the white robe that is the sign of their baptism. In some places the cassock and surplice are used, or an emblem or medallion. The stole is not to be used, since it is a sign of ordination. The white baptismal robe is preferable because it has a long tradition; it covers the distinctions of economic status and gender, is visible at a distance, and has a certain dignity.

There is a great deal of repetition and routine in the distribution of Communion in large assemblies. The words and motions are repeated many times and the danger is that the minister might appear to be uninterested or even bored with this ministry. A kindly facial expression, an inflection of voice, the mention of a name and good eye contact will overcome the

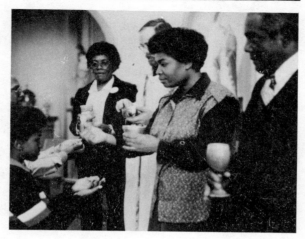

appearance of boredom. A lively faith and internal prayer to Jesus, whose body and blood is being handled, will quickly erase any feelings of routine.

For many ministers in the liturgy, their role is precious to them. Yet, if a person finds that this particular ministry impedes their prayer, they should quietly retire from it and seek another way to minister. Also, it is good to have some Sundays off. The parish should have enough designated Ministers of the Bread and Cup so that they can rotate the responsibility, but not so many that one's turn comes up only rarely. A good rule of thumb might be twice a month at one Mass per week. Of course, there may be exceptions to this.

Some people who minister during the liturgy want to have the opportunity to sit with their families or to observe others doing the ministry. This is a good idea, and it helps to attract others into liturgical ministry. Moreover, as volunteers, liturgical ministers should have a renewable term of service, so that there is a juncture at which they may retire gracefully, or be replaced if their talent for the ministry has faded.

The Parish Worship Committee and the pastor may plan for retreats or days of recollection for the Ministers of the Bread and Cup, as a reward for their generosity and as an invitation to grow in holiness.

Questions
for Reflection
and Discussion

Do you understand the words of Jesus, "Do this in memory of me," which echo through your church week after week, as applying to the Minister of the Bread and Cup? In what ways?

As Minister of the Bread and Cup, in what concrete ways do you express your faith to the assembly? How does the communicant express his or her faith?

What is your reaction, or feeling, to the statement that Ministers of the Bread and Cup are "waiters." Do you like it, or dislike it? Why? Do the ministers in your parish have the same duties as those mentioned in this chapter? More? Fewer? If the latter two, what are they? Why the difference? Are there some duties, as Minister of the Bread and Cup, that you would rather do or not do? Why do you think you feel this way?

Are you offered opportunities for study and prayer so that you may "learn all matters concerning public divine worship and strive to grasp their inner spiritual meaning"?

If the procedure outlined here varies in any substantial manner from your parish practice, it would be helpful to understand the reasons for the differences. Why do you think the celebrant and Ministers of the Bread and Cup consume the sacred breads or hosts after Communion, when they are not abundant?

Does your parish provide you with the opportunity to meet the pastor and the parish council's liturgy committee to discuss and review your ministry? Why do you think this meeting is important? What do you think should be on the agenda for such a meeting? Write out a program for a Day of Recollection for Ministers of the Bread and Cup: the talk and instruction topics, the time slots, the practice opportunities, the prayer opportunities.

The Minister
of Music

Like the usher, the church musician is not a newcomer on the liturgy scene. There have been musicians serving in the liturgy throughout the Christian centuries. Great composers, directors, and choirs have served in the Church. The Mass itself became a musical art form. The question may be asked, Why now should only certain Church musicians be called "Ministers of Music"? Part of the answer, dealt within the first two chapters, lies in the restored understanding of ministry that underlies this book. The other part of the answer lies in a new understanding of the function of 1) leadership in liturgy, and 2) music in liturgy.

Leadership in the Liturgy

A case can be made for the term "Director of the Ministry of Music." Because each member of the assembly is in a sense a minister of music, the leader should not take to himself the total responsibility for carrying out the music. As with the other ministries, the Ministry of Music makes sense only in the context of the assembly. This is clearly understood. As leader, the Minister of Music has a greater gift and a greater responsibility. Not every Church musician or singer is thereby a Minister of Music. The sense of call, the widened responsibility, the evident gift and talent for such service, *and* the ability to lead others are necessary attributes for the Minister of Music.

By parallel, the Minister of Hospitality must be able to lead others to greater sense of belonging and unity; the Minister of the Word must be able to lead others to a greater understanding and appreciation of the Word; the Minister of the Bread and Cup must be able to lead others to frequent and more faith-filled Communion with the Lord. The ones, therefore, who lead others to greater beauty in their musical praise of God are Ministers of Music. "Ministry" means to lead others to God by what we do, that is, witnessing with our very selves in a public, recognized way.

Music in the Liturgy

The function of music in the liturgy is the second part of the answer to why we name only certain people as Ministers of Music. Music must serve the liturgy. The beauty of music contributes to the beauty of the liturgy. Secular music may be quite beautiful and good, but if it doesn't contribute to the common prayer of the assembly, it has no place in the liturgy. Again by parallel with the other ministries: at home, hospitality may mean a cold beer and a warm bed. The Minister of Hospitality would hardly transfer those good hospitable things to the assembly and try to make them fit! The inspirational writings of Ghandi or Kahil Gibran are beautiful and good, but the Minister of the Word would hardly try to propose them as the Word of God to the assembly. The Minister of Music is a faith-filled servant-leader of the people's music at Mass. He or she may minister by vocal music or by instrumental music, with a choir or with the whole assembly.

The impression still lives on in some quarters that music is auxiliary and non-essential to the liturgy. It appears to some as decorative and unnecessary. The typical Mass would be low, that is, all spoken; anything else would be embellishment. If music must be done, then it can be sandwiched into those lulls in the words and actions of the Mass, when people have nothing else to do. The four-hymn Mass comes close to this minimalism.

The Minister of Music leads the sung parts of the Mass by directing the choir (which is considered as part of the assembly), the whole assembly, or by singing solo the antiphonal parts. He or she may also lead by accompanying the song with a musical instrument or by simply playing the instrument as background for reading or meditation.

The priest and deacon also have certain musical parts to sing. The Minister of Music assists them through rehearsal and accompaniment. With the priest-presider, the Minister of Music must sit with the Liturgy Planning Committee to work out the coordination of the many variables in the Mass. Possessing a competent knowledge of a contemporary Church music, the Minister of Music makes a key contribution to the shared decision-making. He or she may serve as musical advisor to the committee.

Within this committee the Minister of Music may find the affirmation that, indeed, the music *is* helping the assembly to pray more beautifully and therefore better. If such a committee does not yet exist, the Minister of Music needs to sample the responses of people regarding the music put before them to sing. In this way, the Minister of Music is a true servant, not imposing his or her tastes upon the assembly, but serving their needs. At the same time, the assembly cannot simply stay with the same old music for lack of visionary leadership.

The Minister of Music must know the pertinent documents and legislation regarding Church music. See the bibliography for references. Also, he or she must use the best printed materials available.

The Minister of Music must be:

1. A Catholic willing to share his or her faith with the assembly.
2. A competent musician.
3. A leader willing to make a commitment to the parish for a period of time.

When Music Is Appropriate

In order of priority, here are the parts of the Mass that are generally to be sung.

The Acclamations:
1. "Alleluia" before the gospel
2. "Holy" before the Eucharistic Prayer
3. Memorial Acclamation after the words of Remembrance
4. Great "Amen" after the Eucharistic Prayer
5. Doxology to the Lord's Prayer

The Processionals:
1. Entrance Song: seasonal, celebrative, recollective
2. Communion Song: simple, eucharistic, joyful

The Responsorial Psalms

The Ordinary Chants:
1. "Lord, Have Mercy": brief litany of praise or penance
2. "Glory to God": hymn of praise; poetic; restricted use: opportunity for the choir
3. Lord's Prayer: community prayer
4. "Lamb of God": opportunity for choir; litany can be extended for the breaking of the bread
5. Profession of Faith: spoken in declamatory fashion

The Supplemental Songs:
1. The Offertory Song: instrumental or choir; not necessarily an "offering" theme
2. The Song After Communion: optional; meditative

3. The Recessional Song: optional; recapitulating, sending forth

The use of intentional silence during parts of the Mass often depends on the decision of the priest-presider and the Minister of Music. Neither will be offended by the other if one suggests silence at a certain time. Good planning will include some silence and a deliberate pacing of one element after another. The Minister of Music gives evidence by his or her prayerful attitude that a certain time is for reflection, not for finding the next piece of music.

Since the field of Church music is rapidly expanding, and sampling and choices have to be made constantly, a large part of the Minister of Music's job is to be in touch with other musicians, to attend regional workshops, and to write to publishers for new material. Music rehearsal is already a prayer and a good service.

The choice of musical instruments is often determined by available talent, the cultural tastes of the people, and finances. The organ has a traditional pre-eminence. Other instruments, properly amplified, may be the guitar, the flute, the clarinet, the piano, the harpsichord, the bass, the violin, and so on.

The success or failure of the Minister of Music in a parish depends equally upon 1) musical ability 2) ability to share one's faith and 3) ability to motivate groups of people. Getting and maintaining volunteers in a choir or guitar group is a time-consuming job. The hours of

rehearsal, and sometimes the repetition of several Masses on a weekend, takes a good deal of time. For these reasons it may be necessary in justice to hire the Minister of Music on a set salary, or stipend. On-going training and education in music and in liturgy – undertaken at parish expense – would also support and strengthen this important ministry in the Church.

Questions
for Reflection
and Discussion

How much does the music at Mass in your parish mean to you? To the parishioners? Is music really important in your parish? Under the pastor, do you know who is responsible for music in your parish?

Does your parish use musical instruments other than organs and guitars, at least occasionally? Do you think it should, at least in principle? Why? Does your parish ask parishioners what they think of the music at Mass? Do you think they should be asked? Why?

Do you agree with the section on when music might be in order at Mass? Why? If your parish practice differs from these norms, is this difference and the reasons for it understood by all the Ministers of Music?

Do you believe that all the Ministers of Music in your parish truly appreciate that regular planning and rehearsal is the only way to come to the high quality that befits the liturgy? If they do not, what should be done about it? Do the ministers appreciate their singular role toward greatly enriching the Sunday Mass for all the assembly? What might be done to deepen this appreciation?

Suggested Reading

Bauman, William. *The Ministry of Music: A Guide for Practicing Church Musicians.* Collegeville, MN: Liturgical Press, 1975.

Bausch, William J. "Ministry, A and The" and "Ministry and Identity" in *The Christian Parish.* Mystic, CT: Twenty-Third Publications, 1980.

Bishops' Committee on the Liturgy. *Environment and Art in Catholic Worship.* Washington, DC: National Conference of Catholic Bishops, 1978.

_____. *Ministries in the Church* (Study Text 3). Washington, DC: National Conference of Catholic Bishops, 1974.

_____. *Music in Catholic Worship.* Washington, DC: National Conference of Catholic Bishops, 1972.

_____. *Rite of Christian Initiation of Adults.* Washington, DC: National Conference of Catholic Bishops, 1974.

Cooke, Bernard. *Ministry to Word and Sacraments: History and Theology.* Philadelphia: Fortress Press, 1976.

Dulles, Avery, S.J. *Models of the Church.* New York: Doubleday, 1974.

Fleming, Austin. "The Animator," *Pastoral Music,* (October-November 1979).

_____. "Are We Ministers of Music or Directors of the Ministry of Music?" *Pastoral Music,* (February-March 1981).

Geaney, Dennis J., O.S.A. "Parish Goldmine: Let's Develop Lay Liturgy Leaders." *Journal of the Liturgical Conference,* (March-April 24 1979).

Henchal, Michael J. *Sunday Worship in Your*

Parish: What It Is, What It Could Be. Mystic, CT: Twenty-Third Publications, 1979.

Henderson, Frank. *Ministries of the Laity.* Ottawa: Canadian Catholic Conference, 1978.

Johnson, Lawrence J. *The Celebrating Community: Word and Eucharist.* Wilmington, DE: Berakah Publications, 1977.

The Liturgy Documents: A Parish Resource (Liturgy Training Program). Chicago: Archdiocese of Chicago, 1980.

Liturgy With Style & Grace: A Basic Manual For Planners & Ministers (Liturgy Training Program). Chicago: Archdiocese of Chicago, 1978.

"Ministries and Liturgy." *National Bulletin on Liturgy,* 9 (March-April 1976). Ottawa: Canadian Catholic Conference.

"Ministries in the Church." *Chicago Studies,* 40 (Summer 1977).

Parish Liturgy Handbook. Baltimore: Archdiocese of Baltimore.

"Sunday Eucharist." *National Bulletin on Liturgy,* 71 (November-December 1979). Ottawa: Canadian Catholic Conference, 1979.

"Sunday Liturgy: When Lay People Preside." *National Bulletin on Liturgy,* 79 (May-June 1981). Ottawa: Canadian Catholic Conference, 1981.

Walsh, Eugene A., S.S. *The Ministry of the Celebrating Community.* Glendale, AZ: Pastoral Arts Associates of North America, 1977.

_____. *Practical Suggestions for Celebrating Sunday Mass.* Glendale, AZ: Pastoral Arts Associates of North America, 1978.

_____. *The Theology of Celebration.* Glendale, AZ: Pastoral Arts Associates of North America, 1977.